D0555971

The Quarter Horse

Rachel Damon Criscione

The Rosen Publishing Group's

PowerKids Press™

New York

To Judy Nevins, a great sister and friend

Published in 2007 by The Rosen Publishing Group, Inc.
29 East 21st Street, New York, NY 10010

First Edition
Editors: Melissa Acevedo and Amelie von Zumbusch
Book Design: Ginny Chu

Photo Credits: Cover, title page © Bob Langrish/Animals Animals; p. 4 © Renee Lynn/Corbis; p. 7 Library of Congress Prints and Photographs Division; p. 8 Sam Savitt.com; p. 11 Cindy Reiman; p. 12 The American Quarter Horse Association; p. 15 © Buddy Mays/Corbis; p. 16 © Mark Peterson/Corbis; p. 19 © Dale C. Spartas/Corbis; p. 20 Photo and pedigree courtesy of Constance Hartman.

Library of Congress Cataloging-in-Publication Data

Criscione, Rachel Damon.
  The Quarter horse / Rachel Damon Criscione.— 1st ed.
      p. cm. — (The Library of horses)
  Includes bibliographical references and index.
  ISBN 1-4042-3448-9 (lib. bdg.)
  1. Quarter horse—Juvenile literature. I. Title.
  SF293.Q3C75 2007
  636.1'33—dc22
                                        2005026679

Manufactured in the United States of America

Table of Contents

Quarter horses are
known for their
speed. They are one
of the fastest kinds of
horse in the world.
They can run down a
straight track at a
speed of 50 to 55
miles per hour
(80–88.5 km/h).

The Most Popular Horse

The American quarter horse is the most popular **breed** of horse in the world. People admire these sturdy horses for their speed, cleverness, and gentle manner.

When the English colonists came to America, they wanted a horse that would work hard on the farm during the week, race on holidays, and take the family to church on Sundays. They **bred** the hardworking quarter horse because they wanted a fast runner. They also wanted a horse that would be easy to handle. The quarter horse gave the colonists just what they needed and wanted.

The quarter horse was named for its ability to run a quarter-mile race faster than any other kind of horse when they were first bred in the 1600s. These horses can go from standing still to a full **gallop** in only a few steps.

All-American Horse

The quarter horse is considered to be the first American breed of horse because it was first bred for use in the American colonies. This horse is the result of breeding the jennet with the Thoroughbred.

When Spanish colonists sailed to North America in the sixteenth century, they brought jennets with them. Jennets were short and strong. English colonists brought Thoroughbred horses with them when they came to the colonies during the seventeenth century. Thoroughbreds were tall, thin, and fast.

The English colonists bred the two horses together. The result was a horse that had the best features of both its parents. This new breed of horse was a strong, average-sized horse that could run very fast. The quarter horse soon became popular throughout the colonies.

Early American colonists bred English Thoroughbreds and Spanish jennets together to create the quarter horse. This horse is a famous Thoroughbred from the 1800s called Lula.

Quarter horse races like this one were popular when America was an English colony. The first American quarter horse races took place in Enrico County, Virginia, in 1674.

Quarter Horses in Early America

Horse racing was a popular sport in England. By the early 1600s, its popularity had spread to the English colonies. The first colonial races were called match races. These were races in which two horses ran a quarter mile (.4 km). The races were usually run along the main street of a town because it was often the only place straight enough and long enough for the horses to run fast. The race was so short that **spectators** standing along the road could see the race, which lasted only seconds, from start to finish.

As settlers began to move west during the 1800s, the hardworking quarter horse moved with them. Quarter horses helped the settlers build new communities by dragging logs, pulling plows, working with cattle, and carrying supplies.

Police Horses

The quarter horse is known for its hard work on farms. However, some specially trained members of the breed can be found today working with police departments in big cities, such as Tokyo, Japan, and New York City. Quarter horses have been working in the Mounted Unit of the New York Police Department (NYPD) since the mid-1800s. The NYPD uses these horses for crowd control, street patrols, and directing **traffic**.

All horses accepted into the Mounted Unit must be smart and able to remain calm when surrounded by crowds, loud noises, and traffic. These horses must also be calm and strong because they must work in all kinds of weather with a lot of people around. These are all features that are found in quarter horses.

The NYPD Mounted Unit was founded in 1871. It still exists today. The unit is used mostly for controlling crowds at major public events.

AMERICAN QUARTER HORSE
COLOR & MARKINGS
REFERENCE CHART

Following are examples of markings and 16 colors recognized by the American Quarter Horse Association. Notice that there may be extreme variations within a color category.

MARKINGS: Star, strip and snip. Left fore half pastern white. Right hind stocking. Left hind pastern white. (Note: This horse's flaxen tail is often found with the sorrel color.)

MARKINGS: Blaze. White on lower lip and chin. Socks on fore feet. Left hind stocking.

MARKINGS: Star. Left hind half pastern white. Right hind sock.

MARKINGS: Blaze. Socks on all feet.

MARKINGS: Left hind coronet white.

Sorrel: Body color reddish or copper-red; mane and tail usually same color as body, but may be flaxen; may have dorsal stripe.

Black: Body color true black without light areas; mane and tail black.

Bay: Body color ranging from tan, through red, to reddish-brown; mane and tail black on lower legs; may have dorsal stripe.

NO MARKINGS

MARKINGS: Right fore pastern white.

RECOGNIZED COLORS

MARKINGS: Hind pasterns white. (Note: The head and lower legs have remained predominantly dark.)

NO MARKINGS

Brown: Body color brown or black with light areas around muzzle, eyes, flank and inside upper legs; mane, tail and points black.

Blue Roan: More or less uniform mixture of white and black hairs on the body, but darker on head and lower legs; can have a few red hairs in mixture.

Grulla: Body color smoky or mouse-colored (not a mixture of black and white hairs, but each hair mouse-colored); mane and tail black; black on lower legs; usually has dorsal stripe.

MARKINGS: Star and strip. (Note: Roaning is primarily on body while head and legs have remained dark.)

NO MARKINGS: (Note: Head and lower legs hair remained dark while roaning is primarily on body.)

MARKINGS: Stockings on hind legs.

MARKINGS: Right fore sock.

Bay Roan: More or less uniform mixture of white with red hairs on a large portion of the body; darker on head, usually red but can have a few black hairs in mixture; black mane and tail and black on lower legs.

Red Roan: More or less uniform mixture of white with red hairs on the body, but red on head and lower legs; red or flaxen mane and/or tail.

Chestnut: Body color dark red or brownish-red; mane and tail usually dark red or brownish-red, but may be flaxen. Mane and tail may appear black, but lower legs will be red; may have dorsal stripe.

NO MARKINGS

MARKINGS: Star and strip. Left hind sock.

MARKINGS: Left hind sock.

Red Dun: A form of dun with body color yellowish or flesh colored; mane and tail are red or reddish, flaxen, white or mixed; has red or reddish dorsal stripe and usually red or reddish zebra stripes on legs and transverse stripe over withers.

Dun: Body color yellowish or gold; mane and tail may be black or brown; has dorsal stripe and usually has zebra stripes on legs, and transverse stripe over withers.

NO MARKINGS

MARKINGS: Left fore half pastern white. (An intermediate stage of the graying effect. This commonly would be called a dappled gray.)

NO MARKINGS: (A relatively young horse with the graying effect most predominant on its head - note that on mane head and lower legs remain dark though body is roaned.)

NO MARKINGS: (An advanced stage of the graying effect, often called flea-bitten gray.)

MARKINGS: Right hind stocking. Dark spots on right hind coronet. (Note that in this horse, the gray characteristic is superimposed over a basic sorrel or chestnut color, making this a gray horse. It is a common characteristic of gray horses to have patches of concentrated white hair which are not objectionable providing there is dark skin underlying the patches.)

MARKINGS: Fore pastern white. Right hind sock.

Palomino: Body color a golden yellow; mane and tail white. Palominos typically do not have dorsal stripes.

Gray: Mixture of white with any other colored hairs; often born solid colored or almost solid colored and gets lighter with age as more white hairs appear; may have dorsal stripe.

Buckskin: Body color yellowish or gold; mane and tail black; usually black on lower legs. Buckskins typically do not have dorsal stripes.

NO MARKINGS

NO MARKINGS

Cremello: Body color white or light cream; mane and tail white; pink or pinkish skin over entire body; blue eyes.

Perlino: Body color white or light cream; mane and tail usually have a darker tint - pale copper or orange; pink or pinkish skin over entire body; blue eyes.

AMERICAN QUARTER HORSE ASSOCIATION

P.O. Box 200, Amarillo, Texas 79168 • (806) 376-4811 • www.aqha.com

This chart, created by the American Quarter Horse Association, shows most of the colors a pure quarter horse can be.

A Powerful Horse

A quarter horse has a strong, powerful build that makes it well suited for riding. Their short, wide backs easily hold a **saddle**. The horse's deep, wide shoulders hold the saddle securely in place, helping riders keep their balance. The horse's strong legs allow it to move its weight easily and to **maneuver** around objects quickly.

Quarter horses come in many colors. Chestnut and bay, or reddish brown, are two of the most common. To be listed with the American Quarter Horse Association (AQHA), a quarter horse can have no white marking above its knees, except on its face.

The average quarter horse weighs about 1,200 pounds (544 kg). It measures between 14 and 16 **hands** (56–64 in) when measured from the ground to its **withers**.

Show Horses and Racehorses

Today the quarter horse can be seen **competing** in English- and Western-style horse shows and at racetracks across the country. The English riding style came to America through early colonists. Western riding is based on the riding styles of Western cowboys who worked on cattle **ranches** in the American West. Although the two riding styles are different, the quarter horse is suited to do both.

Many quarter horses are used as racehorses. One of the most famous quarter horse events is the All-American **Futurity**. It is held each year at Ruidoso Downs, in New Mexico. The race features two-year-old quarter horses, which run a quarter-mile race. This race is called the world's richest quarter horse race because the owner of the winning horse receives more than two million dollars in prize money.

This is a picture of the All-American Futurity horse race. It takes place every Labor Day. Labor Day is the first Monday in September.

This girl is riding a quarter horse at the Pinegrove Dude Ranch Resort in New York's Catskill Mountains. A teacher stands nearby in case the girl needs any help while riding.

Riding a Quarter Horse

Quarter horses are quick to learn. This makes them easy to train. Since quarter horses will do almost anything that a rider asks of them, they are a good choice for beginning riders.

The best way to learn to ride a quarter horse is on a well-trained horse under the watchful eye of a good teacher. When you take lessons at a riding stable, some places might teach you only how to ride. Others will teach you how to **groom** and care for the horse as well.

One of the first things you will learn in a riding lesson is how to keep your balance while sitting in a saddle. Then you will learn to use your voice, hands, legs, and body to show your horse what you want it to do.

"Cow Sense"

The quarter horse is a good horse to use for farmwork, traveling, and racing. It is the quarter horse's "cow sense" that makes it naturally suited to work with cattle. A quarter horse's **instincts** let the horse know just what a cow will do in any given setting.

Sometimes a calf needs to receive drugs to help fight an illness or be **branded**. This is when quarter horses are needed. A cowboy will direct the quarter horse to separate the calf from the herd. The horse will then chase the calf in the proper direction. If the calf tries to get back to the herd, the quarter horse moves with the calf, not allowing it any room to move. This "cow sense" is one reason that many ranchers still prefer a good quarter horse to a jeep or a truck.

This cowboy is chasing a calf while riding a quarter horse. A quarter horse's speed is very helpful to cowboys when they chase calves.

Eagleized 3319339 1994 sorrel gelding

Sire (or father) side of pedigree

The Legal Eagle 1988
2752140 sorrel

Im a Big Leaguer 1982
2696628 chestnut

Barpasser 1970
0683215 chestnut

Johannis 1971
2688699 chestnut

Select Hobby 1980
1682175 sorrel

Reed Cheyenne 1966
0442302 sorrel

Rosy Rita 1972
0833884 sorrel

Dam (or mother) side of pedigree

MS Preference 1986
2444307 sorrel

Reference 1983
2007649 bay

Impressive 1969
0767246 sorrel

Joak Easter Gal 1961
0246495 dun

Miss Whiska Jack 1978
1415867 red roan

Two D Skip 1975
1158875 chestnut

Oh Goodie 1963
0251872 gray

This is a pedigree of Eagleized, a quarter horse. Pedigrees trace the history and bloodlines of an individual horse. The picture above shows Eagleized at a horse show.

Records and Bloodlines

The American quarter horse has been around for a long time. However, it did not become an official breed until 1940. The American Quarter Horse Association was formed that year to keep records on the breeding and accomplishments of American quarter horses. With more than three million horses officially signed up, it is the largest horse breed in the world.

The AQHA only signs up quarter horses that have either a mother or a father that is a known quarter horse. The AQHA keeps records so horse owners can trace the **bloodlines** of their horse. The value of a horse depends on the history of its family. Therefore, a horse that comes from a prizewinning family would be worth more than a horse from a family without winners.

Quarter Horses Today

Today quarter horses are the most popular horse breed in North America. There are more than 2,860,000 quarter horses living in the United States. Some of these quarter horses have important jobs working with police officers. Other quarter horses work on farms or ranches. However, the majority of quarter horses are used for recreational activities. They are a favorite breed among people who compete in both English- and Western-style horse shows across the country.

The quarter horse has come a long way since the English colonists bred their Thoroughbreds with the small Spanish horses they found in America. Though they have been around for hundreds of years, quarter horses continue to be admired for their strength, speed, and beauty.

Glossary

bloodlines (BLUD-lynz) An animal's direct blood relatives, such as its parents.

branded (BRAND-ed) Burned with a hot iron to mark something to show ownership.

bred (BRED) Brought a male and a female animal together so they will have babies.

breed (BREED) A group of animals that look alike and have the same relatives.

competing (kum-PEET-ing) Opposing another in a game or test.

futurity (fyoo-TUR-eh-tee) A race for two-year-old horses in which the entries are picked before birth.

gallop (GA-lup) The fastest pace of a horse.

groom (GROOM) To clean someone's body and make it neat.

hands (HANDZ) A way to measure the height of a horse. One hand is equal to four inches (10 cm), about the width of an adult human hand.

instincts (IN-stinkts) The feelings every creature has that help it know what to do.

maneuver (muh-NOO-ver) To get into or out of a position for a purpose.

ranches (RANCH-ez) Large farms for raising cattle, horses, or sheep.

saddle (SA-dul) A leather seat that is used on the back of a horse to carry a rider.

spectators (SPEK-tay-terz) People who see or watch something but do not take an active part.

traffic (TRA-fik) The cars, airplanes, ships, or people moving along a path.

withers (WIH-therz) A place between the shoulders of a dog or horse.

Index

Web Sites

Due to the changing nature of Internet links, PowerKids Press has developed an online list of Web sites related to the subject of this book. This site is updated regularly. Please use this link to access the list:

www.powerkidslinks.com/horse/quarter/